BERKLEE EAR TRAINING
DUETS AND TRIOS

GAYE TOLAN HATFIELD

Dedicated to my father, Peter J. Tolan

Thanks to Berklee College of Music and my friends and family for their support and encouragement.

BERKLEE PRESS

Editor in Chief: Jonathan Feist
Senior Vice President of Online Learning and Continuing Education/CEO of Berklee Online: Debbie Cavalier
Vice President of Enrollment Marketing and Management: Mike King
Vice President of Academic Strategy: Carin Nuernberg
Editorial Assistants: Emily Jones, Megan Richardson

Music Performed, Recorded, and Engineered by Brad Hatfield
Notation Editing and Initial Typesetting by Wm. C. Brinkley

ISBN 978-0-87639-196-9

Berklee
Press

1140 Boylston Street
Boston, MA 02215-3693 USA
(617) 747-2146

Visit Berklee Press Online at
www.berkleepress.com

Berklee Online

Study music online at
online.berklee.edu

DISTRIBUTED BY

HAL•LEONARD®
7777 W. BLUEMOUND RD. P.O. BOX 13819
MILWAUKEE, WISCONSIN 53213

Visit Hal Leonard Online
www.halleonard.com

Berklee Press, a publishing activity of Berklee College of Music, is a not-for-profit educational publisher.
Available proceeds from the sales of our products are contributed to the scholarship funds of the college.

CONTENTS

INTRODUCTION: HOW TO PRACTICE SIGHTREADING v

    About the Audio vi

    How to Use This Book vi

CHAPTER 1. MAJOR 1

    C Major Duet I 1

    C Major Trio 2

    C Major Duet II 3

    F Major Duet I 3

    F Major Duet II 4

    G Major Duet 5

    G Major Canon 6

    D Major Duet I 7

    D Major Trio 8

    B♭ Major Duet I 9

    B♭ Major Duet II 9

CHAPTER 2. MINOR 10

    A Minor Duet I 10

    A Minor Duet II 11

    D Minor Trio 12

    D Minor Canon 14

    E Minor Duet 15

    C Minor Duet 16

    C Minor Canon 17

    B Minor Duet I 17

    B Minor Duet II 18

    C♯ Minor Trio 18

    G Minor Trio 19

CHAPTER 3. MODES 20

    B♭ Lydian Duet 20

    D♭ Lydian Duet 21

    C Mixolydian Duet 22

    D Mixolydian Duet 23

    G Mixolydian Trio 24

    A Dorian Duet 26

    E Dorian Canon 26

    B Dorian Duet 27

    A Phrygian Duet 28

    D Phrygian Canon 29

CHAPTER 4. CHROMATICS **30**

    C Major Duet III 30

    C Minor Trio 31

    D Major Duet II.. 32

    D Major Duet III 33

    D♭ Major Duet 34

    D Minor Duet... 34

    B♭ Major Duet III 35

    A Major Duet I 35

    E♭ Major Duet 36

    F Major Duet III 36

    E Major Duet 37

CHAPTER 5. COMBINATIONS AND MODULATION **38**

    C Minor Mixed Mode Duet... 38

    D Mixed Mode Trio 39

    A♭ Major Duet I 40

    E♭ Major Mixed Mode Duet 40

    A♭ Major Duet II 41

    A Major Duet II 42

    D Major Mixed Mode Duet 43

    B Minor Mixed Mode Duet 44

    B♭ Minor Duet... 44

    A Minor Mixed Mode Duet 45

    D Aeolian Duet 46

SCALE GLOSSARY.. **47**

ABOUT THE AUTHOR **49**

How to Practice Sightreading

There are a few elements to consider when sightreading a melody. The basics include rhythm, solfège syllables, and pitches. There may also be dynamics and articulations present.

If you follow the steps below, your sightreading will become faster and more accurate over time. It's important that you do the steps in order and are successful with each step before moving on to the next.

Step 1: Know the Theory

Identify the clef, key, and time signature.

Step 2: Rhythm Only

Perform the rhythm of the melody on the syllable *tah*, beginning with a moderately slow tempo. The goal is to perform the entire rhythm without stopping, so don't be afraid to start slowly, and then adjust the metronome accordingly.

Step 3: Solfège Out of Time ("Dry Solfège")

Speak the name of the pitches with solfège syllables, along with a metronome, but do not consider the rhythm of the melody yet. Speak the syllables like you would the words in a paragraph, each syllable spoken at a regular pace without stopping. If there is any hesitation in naming the syllables, keep at it before going to the next step.

Step 4: Solfège In Time

Now, you should be ready to speak the solfège using the rhythm of the melody. Keep it honest by using a metronome. When you can do this step without stopping, you're ready to start singing!

Step 5: Pitches Out of Time

First, warm up with the appropriate scale in the given key. When you're able to sing the scale accurately, sing each note of the melody (in solfège, of course) at regular intervals. For instance, put your metronome on 60 bpm, and sing each note of the melody as if they are all half notes. Remember to always reference Do and the scale to find pitches, especially when there are leaps within the melody.

Do not get the pitches from an instrument; remember that you must be the creator of the pitch, using your inner hearing and your voice.

If you have a tough time with this step, go back and warm up that scale!

Step 6: Performance Time

If you've mastered steps one through five, you should be ready to go. It's okay to start with slower tempos than indicated at first.

And, don't forget the icing on the cake: the dynamics and articulations.

ABOUT THE AUDIO

To access the accompanying audio, go to www.halleonard.com/mylibrary and enter the code found on the first page of this book. This will grant you instant access to every example. Examples with accompanying audio are marked with an audio icon.

HOW TO USE THIS BOOK

Use this book to practice sightreading. Singers and instrumentalists alike will find it useful.

Recordings for all parts are provided, so even if you are working on these materials independently, you can have virtual duet and trio partners and can practice every voice with an ensemble. If possible, practice these pieces with other musicians.

For the best personal musical growth, it is recommended that you practice the six-step method for sightreading and are "performance ready" before listening to or singing along with the recording. The ultimate learning goal is independence, not mimicking or memorization.

When you are ready to sing with the recording(s), choose the alternate part(s) that you'd like for your accompaniment. Each recording begins with a two-measure countoff on the tonic note of the key. For example, on the "B♭ Major Duet in 4/4," you'll hear eight quarter notes played on a B♭ before the music begins.

Have fun, and share your success with friends, classmates, and teachers. Take pride in reaching the next level of musical independence.

CHAPTER 1

Major

C MAJOR DUET I

C MAJOR TRIO

C MAJOR DUET II

F MAJOR DUET I

F MAJOR DUET II

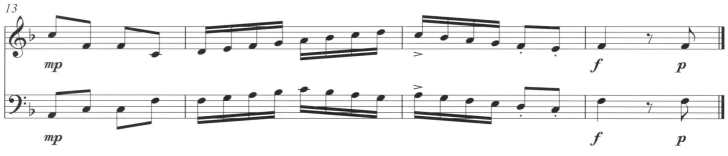

G MAJOR DUET

G MAJOR CANON

When you sing canons, each number indicates where the next voice enters,
singing the melody from the beginning.

D MAJOR DUET I

D MAJOR TRIO

B♭ MAJOR DUET I

B♭ MAJOR DUET II

CHAPTER 2

Minor

A MINOR DUET I

A MINOR DUET II

D MINOR TRIO

D MINOR CANON

E MINOR DUET

C MINOR DUET

♩ = 80

C MINOR CANON

B MINOR DUET I

B MINOR DUET II

C♯ MINOR TRIO

G MINOR TRIO

CHAPTER 3

Modes

B♭ LYDIAN DUET

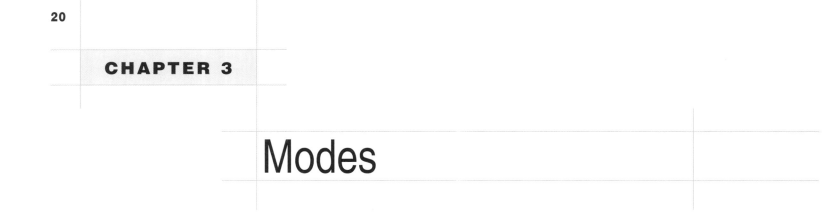

Db LYDIAN DUET

Jazz Waltz ♩ = 112

C MIXOLYDIAN DUET

Funky ♩ = 64

D MIXOLYDIAN DUET

Bossa Feel ♩ = 112

G MIXOLYDIAN TRIO

A DORIAN DUET

E DORIAN CANON

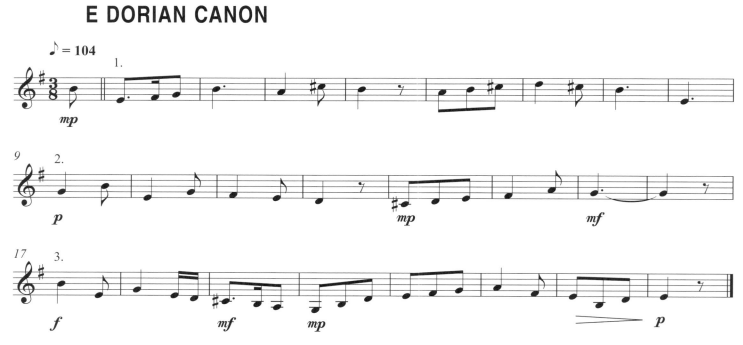

B DORIAN DUET

♩ = 100

A PHRYGIAN DUET

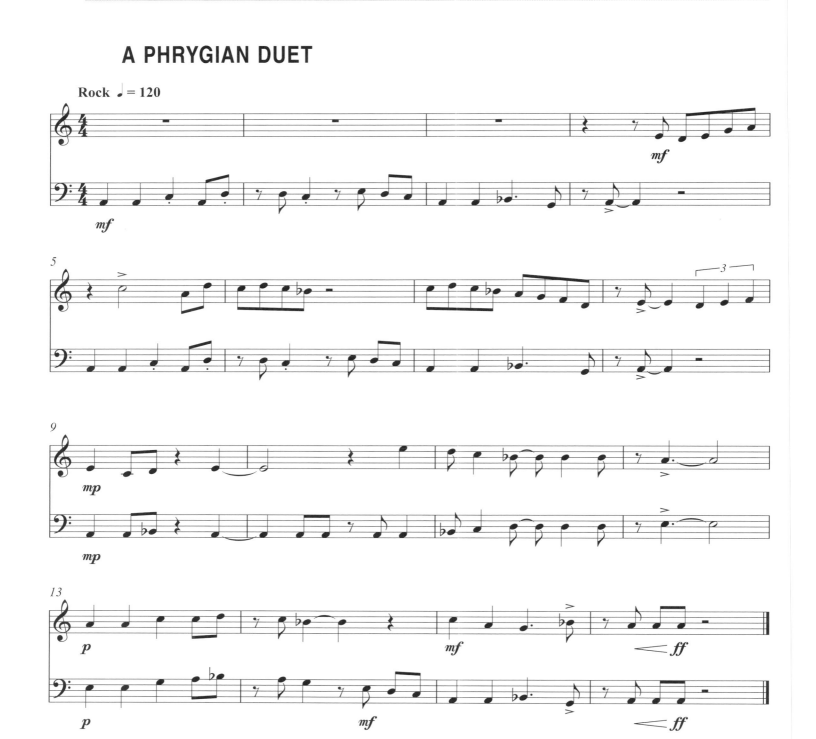

D PHRYGIAN CANON

CHAPTER 4

Chromatics

C MAJOR DUET III

C MINOR TRIO

D MAJOR DUET II

D MAJOR DUET III

D♭ MAJOR DUET

D MINOR DUET

B♭ MAJOR DUET III

Lullabye ♪ = 98

A MAJOR DUET I

♩ = 48

E♭ MAJOR DUET

F MAJOR DUET III

E MAJOR DUET

CHAPTER 5

Combinations and Modulation

C MINOR MIXED MODE DUET

D MIXED MODE TRIO

A♭ MAJOR DUET I

E♭ MAJOR MIXED MODE DUET

A♭ MAJOR DUET II

A MAJOR DUET II

D MAJOR MIXED MODE DUET

B MINOR MIXED MODE DUET

B♭ MINOR DUET

A MINOR MIXED MODE DUET

D AEOLIAN DUET

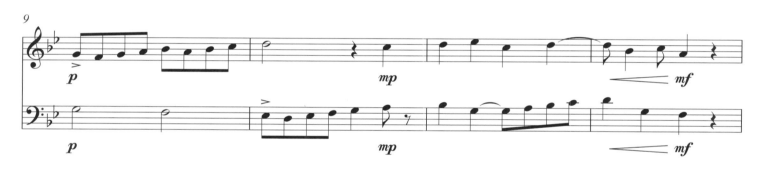

SCALE GLOSSARY

Chapter 1. Major

Major

Do	Re	Mi	Fa	Sol	La	Ti	Do	Ti	La	Sol	Fa	Mi	Re	Do
1	2	3	4	5	6	7	1	7	6	5	4	3	2	1

Chapter 2. Minor

Natural minor

Do	Re	Me	Fa	Sol	Le	Te	Do	Te	Le	Sol	Fa	Me	Re	Do
1	2	♭3	4	5	♭6	♭7	1	♭7	♭6	5	4	♭3	2	1

Harmonic minor

Do	Re	Me	Fa	Sol	Le	Ti	Do	Ti	Le	Sol	Fa	Me	Re	Do
1	2	♭3	4	5	♭6	♮7	1	♮7	♭6	5	4	♭3	2	1

Jazz melodic minor

Do	Re	Me	Fa	Sol	La	Ti	Do	Ti	La	Sol	Fa	Me	Re	Do
1	2	♭3	4	5	♮6	♮7	1	♮7	♮6	5	4	♭3	2	1

Traditional melodic minor

Do	Re	Me	Fa	Sol	La	Ti	Do	Te	Le	Sol	Fa	Me	Re	Do
1	2	♭3	4	5	♮6	♮7	1	♭7	♭6	5	4	♭3	2	1

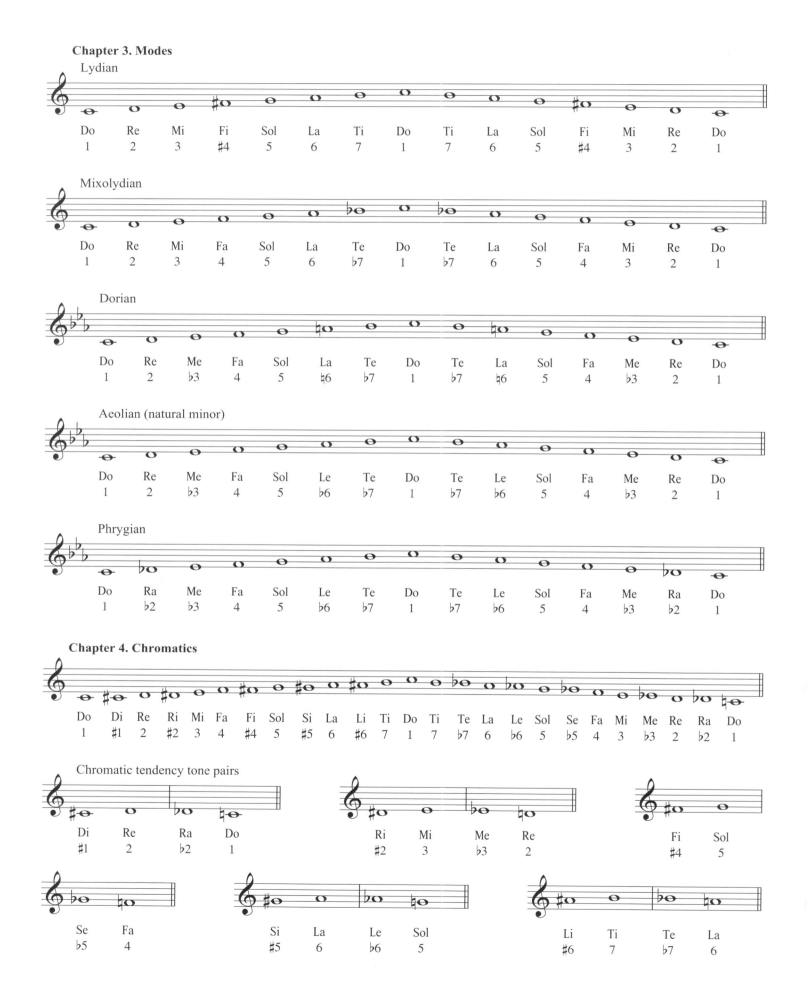

ABOUT THE AUTHOR

Photo by Kiki Larouge Photography

Gaye Tolan Hatfield is a professor in the Ear Training Department at Berklee College of Music, where she has also taught in the Harmony, Ensemble, and Vocal Departments. She is also a course instructor and author for Berklee Online.

Gaye has been an active vocalist, flutist, and arranger in the Boston area since the 1980s. She has earned four Daytime Emmy nominations as part of the composing team for *The Young and the Restless* on CBS. Her arrangements have also been performed by the Tanglewood Festival Chorus and on NPR's *From the Top*.